The Splendour of
NEW ZEALAND

Photography by Chris Swan

CLB 1321
Published in New Zealand 1986 by Gordon & Gotch (NZ) Ltd.
© 1986 Illustrations and text: Colour Library Books Ltd., Guildford,
    Surrey, England.
Text filmsetting by Acesetters Ltd., Richmond, Surrey, England.
Printed and bound in Barcelona, Spain.
ISBN 0 86283 398 1
Dep.Leg. B- 43.315-85

The Splendour of
NEW ZEALAND

Text by
IVOR MATANLE

WATTLE

A Country of Contrasts

If an ancient wizard had transported the mountains and lakes of Switzerland, the coastline of Norway, the rushing rivers of Scotland and England's rich farmland to the South Pacific, on the other side of the world from Europe, and had there rebuilt them like a primaeval jigsaw puzzle, he might almost have created New Zealand. Yet there would still have been many pieces missing. For New Zealand is unique; a cluster of islands inhabited by little more than three million people, far from anywhere, with a climate that is not tropical yet hardly temperate; a land of lush evergreen trees and plants that are not seen elsewhere; a country whose volcanic origins and inheritance are revealed in pumice, geysers and boiling mud.

To people from more populous countries, New Zealand seems remote; the last stop on a voyage to nowhere. Just two main islands, a few smaller islands and their nearby islets, some 1,200 miles South-East of Australia, separated by over 1,000 miles of sea from the nearest land, and vying with Patagonia and Southern Chile for the honour of being the earth's southernmost permanently inhabited land area, New Zealand relishes its isolation. High on the northernmost point of the North Island is a signpost which reads 'Bluff 745 miles; Equator 2,065 miles; Sydney 1,065 miles; Suva 1,030 miles; Panama 6,579 miles'. As that distance to Bluff, in the extreme South of the country on the Foveaux Strait between the South Island and Stewart Island indicates, New Zealand is far from small. It is in fact of a similar size to Italy, long and narrow, with a land area of 103,376 square miles and a length, if the two islands are taken together, of about a thousand miles. At their widest, the islands are little more than 280 miles across. Between the two is Cook Strait, less than twenty miles wide and named after the redoubtable Yorkshire captain who first charted this land.

According to Maori legend, the South Island is the petrified remains of the great canoe that brought their god-hero Maui to the islands, and the North Island is the sea-monster that he raised from the deep. Certainly, the two islands are sharply different, both in their natural topography and vegetation, and in the way that they have developed under the impact of imported civilisation. The North Island, with its dramatically convoluted coastline, boasts volcanic springs and geysers, hidden bays and a great peninsula stretching North, pointing its finger towards the distant Solomon Islands and New Guinea. At the point where the Northland Peninsula joins the wider body of the North Island, at an isthmus only a few hundred yards wide, stands Auckland, New

Zealand's largest city and its principal seaport. Once the seat of New Zealand's government, and with a population of over half a million in its metropolitan area, Auckland is the major centre of many of New Zealand's industries.

Around Auckland, and for a hundred miles South of the city, the land is comparatively flat. But then the traveller heading South comes upon a dramatic change, as mountainous ridges rising to between three and nine thousand feet rear their rumbling boiling heads above him. For here are most of the volcanic marvels of New Zealand; Lake Taupo, the world's largest volcanic lake, and the result of a volcanic upheaval just a few thousand years ago; and Rotorua, where, in Whakarewarewa Thermal Reserve, one of the geysers shoots jets of hot water to a height of almost a hundred feet and visitors gaze at swirling pools of bubbling hot mud. Rotorua golf course claims as its unique quality jets of steam issuing from fissures about the fairways, a piece of golfing lore comparable to the local rule at Jinja golf club in Uganda during colonial rule, by which a ball resting in a hippo's footmark was deemed to have encountered a natural hazard. Some of the steam beneath the soil of the North Island is put to practical and cost-saving use, since engineers have proved it possible to raise through bore holes large volumes of steam at pressures of over 200 pounds per square inch to power turbine generators.

The volcanic belt in the North Island is some 20 miles wide and 150 miles long, an area of pumice and of rocks encrusted with calcium and silicon from the evaporated water of the geysers. To its West is the excitingly wild coast of the Tasman Sea; to its East the beauty of the Pacific and Hawke Bay. At the Southern tip of the island is Wellington, the capital of New Zealand, and the centre of its agricultural trade. Wellington, although smaller than Auckland, with a population within the city of something over 150,000 – more than 300,000 if one includes the neighbouring city of Hutt Valley – seems closer to the heartbeat of New Zealand as a nation, and is but a short trip across the Cook Strait from the South Island. Although two-thirds of New Zealand's population, and much of its industry, lie in the North Island, most of its electrical power is generated in the South Island, and high-voltage direct-current transmission lines and an undersea cable transmit power across the Strait to the North.

The scenery of the Western side of the South Island is spectacular, recreating much of the grandeur of the European Alps and the Rocky Mountains of the USA. South-West of the largest city of the South Island, Christchurch, are the Southern Alps, first sighted by a Dutch explorer, Abel Tasman, in 1642, charted 127 years later by Captain James Cook, and first settled by immigrants in the 1850s. Appropriately the range is dominated in the North by Mount Cook, New Zealand's highest mountain, which at 12,349 feet looms above the competing grandeur of Mount Tasman and Mount Dampier, both over 11,000 ft, and of Malte Brun to its North-East, and Mount Hooker to its South-West. Here is the 173,000 acre Mount Cook National Park, one of ten such parks in New Zealand which together occupy some 8% of the total area of the country, and a centre for skiing on innumerable snowfields from July to September every year. For Mount Cook, called Aorangi, or 'cloud-piercer' by the Maoris, is only one of 223 mountainous peaks on the South Island. It has the reputation of being a beautiful killer, for many climbers have died on its icy slopes, which are honed to glistening, glass-like smoothness by whipping sub-zero gales. Mountaineers train here for the toughest climbs in the world, and it was on Mount Cook that Sir Edmund Hillary trained for his successful first ascent of Everest in 1953.

To the Eastern side of the South Island lie the Canterbury Plains, New Zealand's largest area of lowland, and one of the country's principal agricultural areas, presided over by the city of Christchurch. In this part of New Zealand, farmers grow wheat, oats and barley, in addition to rearing sheep and cattle for meat, dairy products and wool,

and it is in this area that the country also produces much of the sufficient supply of vegetables and fruit that it grows for its domestic needs. Because the South Island experiences lowland frosts in winter, fruit farmers there are able to grow raspberries, and stone fruits are harvested in Central Otago and on the North Island. Apples are produced around Nelson, at the Northern end of the South Island, and in the area of Hawke Bay on the Eastern side of the North Island, and grapes are grown for wine in the Henderson Valley. But there is no disguising the fact that New Zealand's is an economy based on the Romney sheep, and that the raising of livestock is of major importance to the country's prosperity. New Zealand is the world's third largest producer of wool, after Australia and the Soviet Union, and there are almost 10 million cattle and 55 million sheep in the two principal islands, with more than four-fifths of the cattle and over half of the sheep being raised on the North Island. As a general principle, the wetter areas on the Western side of the country favour cattle, and the drier lands of the East are more suited to sheep.

On the West Coast of the South Island, inching its way to within 900 feet of the Tasman Sea before melting, is the extraordinary Franz Josef Glacier, which somehow contrives to bring glacial ice into a sub-tropical rain forest. But even this cannot compete for sheer scenic beauty with the tortuously mountainous coast of the three million acres of Fiordland National Park, where innumerable fiords and deep rocky fissures carved far into the land create some of the world's most beautiful waterfalls, cascading into tree-lined sounds and tumbling, foaming rivers. Perhaps the most spectacular and unforgettable of these great inlets is Milford Sound, into which the amazing Sutherland Falls drop 1,904 feet to the head of the channel, with sheer rock faces all around. There are many other falls of quite breathtaking scale and grandeur – look for the Bowen Falls and the Upper Bowen Falls particularly. The nearby rain forest receives some two hundred inches of rain every year.

The South Island boasts many other features of great beauty, not least the range of mountains South of the Southern Alps known as the Remarkables, to the South of which is the nineteenth century gold-rush town of Queenstown, close by Lake Wakatipu. The stone buildings of Queenstown, houses and churches alike, cater now for fewer than 2,000 local people during the winter, although, in the height of the gold fever a century and a quarter ago, there were over 10,000 people living in the town. This apparent scarcity of population is more than compensated for by the huge influx of holiday visitors in summer, which swells the population to around 25,000 during the sunnier months, despite the fact that water-skiing on Lake Wakatipu can be an alarmingly chilly enterprise, even in hot weather. Like most of the South Island, this is sheep-rearing country – the fact that there are more sheep in the North Island than there are in the South being explained by the more mountainous terrain of the South Island. Sheep stations or 'runs' in the High Country, as New Zealanders tend to call the rugged 500-mile long mountainous backbone of the South Island, are typically of between 25,000 and 40,000 acres, with between 6,000 and 10,000 head of sheep plus a modest number of cattle. It is not so many years since the hardy New Zealanders working these stations lived rough and carried their drinking water winter and summer, and life in the High Country remains tough. The children of families working in the High Country and in other remote areas of the country are provided with their early education by means of a state-run correspondence school scheme, one of the only such governmentally-organised education-by-mail plans in the world. Transport in these remote agricultural areas was far from easy until the advent of the modern light aircraft and, even now, getting to the nearest town can be a major undertaking for the less well-off workers on the sheep stations. Even with modern equipment and transport, New Zealand is one of Earth's more exciting and challenging wildernesses, a land fit for those who dared.

A Little History

To this demi-paradise of startling visual contrasts came, in the early years of our millenium, a handsome race of light-brown skinned Polynesian people, skilled in the arts of seamanship in their outrigger canoes. According to Maori legend, the first Maori settlers arrived in New Zealand some twenty-five generations ago in a great colonising fleet, but science, that great destroyer of romantic notions, has shown that there were, in fact, two Polynesian civilizations in prehistoric New Zealand. One of these was already present in the Stone Age, and survived by the hunting of the moa, New Zealand's great extinct flightless bird. The other was the later culture which was discovered by the European colonisers, many centuries later. Carbon dating has shown that there were Polynesians settled along the Eastern New Zealand coastline in about 1000 AD, and it is probable that the legend of the great fleet in about 1350 AD was born amidst the excitement of new arrivals to swell the most successful civilisation in Polynesia rather than in the founding of a nation.

This pre-Pakeha ('Pakeha' is a Maori word meaning 'white' or 'spook') civilisation, before the white man came from Europe, was the most successful in Polynesia, with an advanced agriculture which grew, as well as the sweet potato, the yam and the taro root for food, and flax for clothing and basket-weaving. They hunted the native flightless birds for food, fished, and, from time to time, ate each other with considerable relish, for the Maoris were perhaps the ultimate cannibal culture. Few shipwrecked sailors lived to tell the tale, and villages even maintained pens in which to fatten up hapless prisoners until an appropriate moment for their culinary demise. Every Maori had a strong sense of family, which extended beyond his immediately determinable close relatives to assumed kinship with all members of his tribe through a set of supposed common ancestors who, it would be claimed, had all arrived in the same canoe. Each of the ancestral canoes had a name, and Maoris could, and in some cases still can, claim their descent from a given canoe.

The nineteenth century was, in New Zealand as in many other areas of the world, a century of uncertain progress punctuated by wars and unrest, as the white settlers sought, often unfairly, to lay claim to lands which had for centuries been the Maori homelands. One of the earliest exponents of organised warfare against the white colonisers was a chief named Te Rauparaha, who, in 1818, led his tribe South from its home near Auckland in a series of ferociously bloody battles which brought him to an island near Wellington, where he proceeded to acquire large quantities of firearms from British and American whalers. Thus equipped he set about the settlers of the South Island, supplementing his tribe's rations by encouraging them to eat those they killed as they went. A particularly ferocious episode at Akaroa in 1829, when Te Rauparaha sacked the town and carried off most of its inhabitants to be tortured and killed, resulted in mounting pressure for formalisation of British rule, and, in 1840, Te Rauparaha was one of the chiefs who signed the Treaty of Waitangi, which conceded sovereignty to the British Crown. Three years later he was in jail for resisting British acquisition of land, but was released after eighteen months by Governor George Grey, an English military man who, while turning a brisk profit for the Crown by buying Maori land cheap and selling it to settlers at high prices, gained the respect of the Maori people by learning their culture and writing about their traditions and proverbs. Grey built hospitals and schools, virtually put an end to intertribal warfare, and introduced large numbers of Maoris to the benefits of commercial cultivation of the crops they already grew for their own consumption.

Almost Grey's last act before being transferred in 1853 to perform similar minor miracles in Cape Town was to provide New Zealand, almost out of thin air, with the democratic constitution of 1852. Only twelve years after the Treaty of Waitangi, New Zealand was virtually self-governing. However, the peace was not to last. By 1858, the Maoris, who had originally interpreted the Treaty of Waitangi as being for the protection of their property and rights, were enraged by the forced sales of their lands to settlers, and gathered to form the first Maori Nation, with an elected king, in the area South of Auckland still known as the King Country. In 1860, war broke out, and Maoris burned settlers' farmhouses. Three thousand troops and militia replied in kind, burning a Maori village, and there followed a series of minor battles. Faced with rebellion on some scale, the London government summoned Governor George Grey back to New Zealand to take charge. He at first tried a mixture of threats and conciliation, but fighting broke out again at Taranaki in 1863, and General Duncan Cameron was ordered into the King Country, where the Maoris held out valiantly for three days before charging out in the face of

gunfire. Many were killed, and for the moment it seemed that the war was over, which it might have been but for the emergence of a curious Christian heresy called 'hau hau' among the Maoris.

The 'hau hau' belief was based on claims that a vision of the Archangel Gabriel had confirmed to Maori believers that Christianity and cannibalism were compatible, and that chanting 'hau hau' while worshipping in the Christian tradition would render the worshippers immune to bullets. Thus fortified by pious misbelief, and by anger at further endorsement by Parliament of the confiscation of Maori lands, the Maoris fought on until 1866, and, in scattered pockets, mainly in the King Country, until 1872. By then it was clear that bullets were not deflected by incantation, that the Maoris had lost both the war and their lands, and that their historic place in the islands they loved was to be taken not by the white man, but by his sheep.

In 1877, Grey, who had returned to London for twelve years after the wars, was back in New Zealand. He was angry at the abolition of the provincial governments that had formed a key part of his 1852 constitution, and, having run for Parliament in 1876, was Prime Minister, and back in the seat of power. He used his power forcefully and well, pushing through a massive programme of humanitarian reforms – universal education, manhood suffrage, and the triennial election of Parliament were just three – and founding the Liberal Party, before being unseated from power by the land lobby.

There is not room in these pages for a detailed look at the fascinating political history of New Zealand since the Maori Wars, but it is worth noting that much of the success of New Zealand in attracting entrepreneurial investment at the turn of the century and after was due to the advanced fiscal and welfare policies of the Liberal governments. The Liberals removed property taxes on everything but land, introduced a graduated income tax, and passed cheap-loan acts which enabled small farmers to borrow money interest-free. An Industrial Conciliation and Arbitration Act removed the need for strikes, and conditions of labour were guaranteed. State pensions for the aged were introduced in 1898. With the success of these measures in attracting both immigrants and investment, and the success of the sheep-rearing industry, New Zealand grew quickly until the beginnings of world turmoil and the advent of the First World War, followed by the turbulent twenties and the depression.

During the Second World War, New Zealand troops played a prominent part in the fight against the dictators in the European and North African theatres, and the New Zealand meat and dairy industry was a bastion of the Allied larder. It was not until 1968 that the Union Jack, the flag of the United Kingdom, ceased to be seen at all National Party meetings. For New Zealand, although a full and active member of the British Commonwealth of Nations, is truly independent in the second half of the twentieth century, and has recently shown increasing signs of isolationism in world politics.

A Closer Look at New Zealand's Cities

There is an old saw that Dunedin and Christchurch live on last year's income, Wellington lives on this year's income, and Auckland lives on next year's income, and in this trite and obviously overstated aphorism there is a grain of truth. For, as another saying has it, Dunedin was founded by Presbyterians, Christchurch by Anglicans, Wellington by merchants and Auckland by pirates. The differences of style, approach, manner and customs between the cities of New Zealand are in many ways dramatic and self-perpetuating, for it tends to remain in the nature of Presbyterians not to approve of a piratical approach to commerce, and in the attitudes of those with a pragmatic view of life to find pious restraint inhibiting. However such differences of style are easily over-stated; they exist similarly between Glasgow and Edinburgh, New York and Boston, Tel Aviv and Jerusalem.

Dunedin

Founded in 1848 by a nephew of Robert Burns, just eight years after the first settlers sent by the New Zealand Company had arrived at the time of the signing of the Treaty of Waitangi and the proclamation of British sovereignty on May 21st 1840, Dunedin is the smallest of the country's four metropolitan areas, with a 1976 population of 113,500. It lies, surrounded to landward by the fruit-growing province of Otago, at the end of a narrow gulf on the South-East coast of the South Island, and was initially colonised by three hundred fervently Christian settlers belonging to the Free Kirk of Scotland. These settlers endeavoured as a deliberate policy to reproduce in their new home the pattern of life that had prevailed in Britain, seeking to set up overnight a squirearchical rural community in which they could preserve class differences by artificially pegging the price of land, and encouraging arable farming rather than the creation of sheep runs for entirely idealistic reasons. However, progress, in the form of the 1860 gold rush and a large number of immigrants, many of whom were Irish and antipathetic to the intensely puritan Scottish outlook, doomed this experiment in anachronistic social engineering to failure. The immigrants, by their adventurous nature, were more interested in wealth, sheep and commerce than poverty, corn and religion, and, by the time the gold rush ended, a more balanced view of society prevailed.

Today, although it remains true that Presbyterians outnumber Anglicans two to one in Otago, the reverse of the ratio in most other parts of the country, Dunedin is a prosperous if somewhat staid city, with less industrial importance to the country's economy than it once enjoyed, and an air of lost grandeur. The University of Otago, founded in 1861, houses New Zealand's principal medical school and, elsewhere in Dunedin, a rich heritage of rather severe Victorian buildings bears witness to the efforts of the founding fathers, but serves also to emphasise how inappropriate to the modern world their vision has become.

Christchurch

Possessor of New Zealand's oldest newspaper, *The Christchurch Press*, which has been recording the doings of this South Island city for a century and a quarter, Christchurch is as English as Dunedin used to be Scottish, and is both a larger and a lighter, more colourful city than Dunedin, two hundred miles to the South. Founded at the inspiration of colony-maker Edward Gibbon Wakefield when the nineteenth century was just half gone, Christchurch owes, symbolically at least, its origins to 'the Canterbury Pilgrims'. This party of seven hundred and seventy three English settlers, who arrived during 1850 in what are now referred to as 'The First Four Ships' – the *Sir George Seymour*, the *Cressy*, the *Charlotte Jane* and the *Randolph*, were, in fact, half of the first group of some fifteen hundred immigrants from the Old Country, and many were comparatively wealthy people. The Pilgrims had bought land for their settlement, and the money from their investment, and that of the thousands of immigrants who followed them, was used to create the beginnings of the city that visitors admire today.

Christchurch is, in the geographical sense, a city of the plains, close to the extinct volcanoes of Banks Peninsula, yet it is, to the visitor, a city of industry, of flowers and of slightly less than ancient antiquity. Everything is extremely English, from the Anglican Cathedral, tall and Gothic beneath its 240-foot-high spire in Cathedral Square, to the modern campus of Canterbury University. It is New Zealand's second biggest city, with relatively few tall buildings and plenty of attractive leisure facilities – in fact, a city capable of enjoying itself, particularly on the forty miles of beaches that lie to the North around Pegasus Bay

Wellington
At the extreme Southern tip of the North Island and facing the Cook Strait, Wellington must have some claim to be the windiest capital city in the world. Built along the shores of a picturesque, almost circular bay some six miles across with only a narrow exit to Cook Strait, Wellington is a city of visual images, much like San Francisco. It has steep hills and cliffs, steps where there would normally be streets, even cable cars. As New Zealand's capital, it has, as capital cities inevitably have, more than its fair share of civil servants and politicians, but they are not allowed to spoil the atmosphere of intellect and concern for the arts which pervades this more than any other city of New Zealand. In fact, the city's constitutional status contributes to its cosmopolitan air, bringing overseas diplomatic families to the cafés, and to the occasional concerts and theatrical productions which do their best to belie New Zealand's hard-won reputation world-wide as a cultural desert. It is in Wellington more than anywhere else that one realises how little chance New Zealanders usually have of hearing languages other than English spoken in their beautiful country. For only here is it likely that you will hear French, German or Spanish on the streets.

The older buildings in Wellington are predominantly built of timber, and visitors should not miss the delightful Cathedral Church of St. Paul, or the entertainingly eccentric old Government office building, said to be the world's largest wooden structure. Alongside the buildings and narrow streets of the Wellington of the past have grown up high-rise modern offices and commercial buildings, hotels and commercial centres, much like those of other prosperous cities in industrialised countries around the world, and an expressway which finally overcame the problem of there being only two main routes out of the city. Wellington has grown; has to some extent become normalised – but it remains the most interesting of New Zealand's cities. You can get there from the South Island by boarding the ferry from Christchurch, a daily sailing taking several hours, but worth the experience.

Auckland
Far to the North of Wellington, beyond the volcanic belt, stands the greatest city of these islands, Auckland. Unlike the other cities, it is not predominantly English or Scottish, but is a happily free-thinking and commercially-inclined mixture of races and peoples, with a population in its Metropolitan Area of well over 600,000 people. The city is large not only in population terms, but also in sheer geographical spread. The constant risk – even expectation – of earthquakes meant that a very large proportion of houses were built as bungalows, and it was (and to some extent still is) a positively imperative social requirement that a house, if the owner was not to suffer loss of status, should be built on at least a quarter of an acre. The result is a quite remarkable suburban sprawl, creating a city which is over thirty miles in one direction by more than twenty in the other.

Most of New Zealand's town-dwelling Maoris live in Auckland, and the Maori community makes up some 10% of the total population of the Metropolitan Area. Add to this some 40,000 other Polynesian residents, many of them temporary visiting workers from the Island Territories, and it becomes clear that Auckland is the greatest centre of Polynesian culture in the world. For this reason it is in Auckland that you will find the most interesting museums and collections of Maori artifacts, and in Auckland that you will be most likely to see Polynesians about the city in their traditional costumes.

Auckland is one of the few ports in the world that can claim harbours on two different seas. Because the city is built on an isthmus, it is able to use its Western harbour, on the Tasman Sea, for light-draft sailings for Australia, and its Eastern harbour, Waitemata, on the Pacific Ocean, for larger, long-haul vessels. The city is also unusual for requiring its pedestrians to keep left of a centre line on the sidewalk.

Commercially, Auckland is the centre of the meat exporting trade, with the country's principal cold stores and freezing plants, and provides much of the storage for New Zealand's wool trade. As might be expected of a comparatively large city, it has many industries, including steel, chemicals and fertilizer plants and a variety of new technology manufacturing springing up in the wake of the microprocessor revolution. But there can be no doubt that, as with so much else in New Zealand, the economy of Auckland is heavily dependent on sheep. So let us return to the wide open spaces – not this time to agriculture, but to the natural flora and fauna of one of the world's most beautiful countries.

The Wildlife and Plants

Trees and forests
Before the white man came to New Zealand, much of the country was covered with dense rain forests, made up almost entirely of lush evergreen trees and ferns with broad, thick, pulpy leaves. Most of New Zealand's native trees were unknown elsewhere, notably the curiously prehistoric-looking ponga (pronounced 'punga'), a giant fern whose silver underleaf has become a national symbol of New Zealand. The ponga is still found in large numbers, usually at the edge of forest areas in the national parks. The kauri, another exclusively New Zealand species, and now a protected tree, is an evergreen that grows thick and straight as high

as sixty feet without branching, making possible the cutting of planks as wide as seven feet. It was for decades the traditional timber used for the building of fine houses, and is excellent both for carving and for polishing. Other native softwoods, which still grow plentifully in the more mountainous areas, are the rimu, the miro and the matai.

Other trees, notably the southern beech, were similar to species found in many other areas of the world, and grew in great numbers. Still others were thought to be exclusive to Australasia and were then discovered by botanists also to exist in other areas. A notable example of this is the lancewood tree, which has proved to grow also in South America. The forests of New Zealand were central to the Maori economy and culture in pre-Pakeha days, providing plenty of kereru, or wood-pigeon, and other birds for food, and the timber to build houses, food-stores, palisades and canoes, but, sadly, the arrival of European settlers heralded a great change, not only for the forests, but also for the Maoris.

The destruction of the forests had in fact begun long before the white man arrived, when the early Polynesian settlers had set areas of forest afire to drive the great flightless moas on to their spears, and also, on occasion, to make clearings for settlement. But major deforestation started when a trade developed in ships' spars early in the nineteenth century. New Zealand's forests, plentifully endowed with fine hardwoods, seemed to the white settlers to have an endless supply of ideal timber for shipbuilding and repair, and the effect on the historic forests was devastating. After 1850, as large-scale white immigration began, a further reason emerged for the felling of the forests – the clearance of land for agriculture, and the building of homes. Expertise in the handling and processing of timber inevitably led to a flourishing timber trade in its own right, but not until the early twentieth century, when three quarters of the historic forest areas had been eliminated, was the timber industry put on a scientifically managed basis. In fact, it was not until after the Second World War that it became normal for a New Zealand home to be built of anything but wood, and even now many apparently brick-built houses are actually timber-framed and faced with a brick-finish cladding.

Parallel with the felling of the ancient forests, the Europeans imported a great many new species of tree that had not previously grown in the isolated islands of New Zealand. From Europe came pines, poplar and willow, and from Australia the ubiquitous blue gum. The imported species are, in most cases, faster growing than the native trees, and are therefore more economic for growing as shelter on farms or for timber. Since the period between the two world wars, extensive forests of 'exotic' (i.e. non-native) trees have been planted for eventual felling as timber, or for the paper industry, and so well has this been done that New Zealand is now the proud possessor of the largest man-made forests in the world. The biggest of these plantations are in the Golden Downs region, South of Nelson, on South Island, and in the Kaingaroa and Tokoroa areas between the Rangitaiki and Waikato rivers, near Rotorua, North Island. Many ornamental trees have also been planted in New Zealand's cities, for it is probably true that no other country in the world sets such store by plants, flowers and trees within its cities. Along with the imported species of tree have come other plants, some of which, originally introduced as decoration, have discovered that they like the place and have spread like wildfire, becoming a pest to farmers. Principal among these are the gorse and the bramble.

In the coastal areas – of which, because of its abnormally tortuous, and therefore long, coastline, New Zealand has more than its fair share – there are many attractive trees, most of then brilliantly colourful. The pohutukawa and the taupata are able to withstand the often windy and inclement coastal weather, and along the edges of the Northland tidal estuaries are mangrove swamps, not unlike those that characterise parts of the Florida coastline. The Maoris call the mangrove 'manawa'. Some of the best of New Zealand's modern forest scenery is to be found in the Fiordland of the far South-West. Here, the original forestation of New Zealand is very much less disturbed and spoiled than in other areas of the country, and the combination of ancient forest with towering crags, tumbling waterfalls of impressive height and romantic lakes is irresistible.

Two quite remarkable native plants to the New Zealand landscape that should not go unmentioned are the kiwi fruit, or Chinese gooseberry, and the extraordinary cabbage tree. The size of a large plum, the kiwi fruit tastes a little like a pear, and contains slightly alarming-looking black seeds which are eaten with the even more disconcerting green flesh. The cabbage tree might be said to be a Welshman's idea of heaven – a tree whose spiky shoots, when cooked, taste like leeks.

The animals

New Zealand was, before the arrival of the pakehas, almost entirely without native mammals (other than man). There were and are no snakes, and the sole mammal was a form of bat. By way of compensation for this curious omission, which occurred simply because New Zealand's isolation was established before the mammals and marsupials had developed on earth, nature provided the islands with a quite remarkable variety of flightless birds – more than in any other area of the world. Greatest among these was the moa, a heavy cumbersome bird much hunted for food by the early settlers, and finally made extinct by the introduction of firearms. Of the surviving flightless birds, the most important is the little brown kiwi, the bird about the size of a chicken from which white New Zealanders acquired their worldwide nickname. The kiwi is seldom seen in the wild, since it is nocturnal, rare, secretive and inclined to stay in the forest, finding the grubs and worms on which it feeds with a long curved slender bill. Extraordinarily, the kiwi lays eggs that are five inches long and weigh a quarter of its own weight (a comedian once observed that this fact might account for the kiwi's occasional strangled cry).

The eccentricity of New Zealand's bird life knows few bounds. One of its almost flightless species of parrots is a curious creature known as a kakapo, which is given to climbing trees beak over talon, and then gliding in one magnificently ungainly swoop to any convenient point within range before repeating the whole procedure, apparently for no better reason than its own entertainment. Another parrot, far from flightless, is the kea, which has the grisly habit of eating sick sheep alive by using its formidable beak to rip away chunks of flesh. It is also reputed to have kleptomaniac tendencies, stealing anything that looks interesting, and to be mischievous enough occasionally to let car tyres down, but that reputation may owe more to the dry New Zealand sense of humour than to the bird's proclivities.

Other orders of native creatures are also, in many cases, decidedly unusual. Where else would you find a cricket with a fourteen-inch legspread, or a lizard with no penis and the ability to live without breathing for a periods of an hour or more?

Into this curious residue of apparently discarded celestial prototypes, the white man saw fit in the eighteenth and nineteenth centuries to introduce a number of familiar creatures from 'the old country'. As in Australia, rabbits denuded pastures and rapidly became a scourge. Predators such as weasels and stoats, brought in to reduce the rabbit population, instead discovered that they liked kiwis and other creatures which had no developed defence against such vicious carnivores. Man introduced rats and mice, opossums from Australia, deer which stripped the trees, pigs, goats – the list is long. Of course, not all the creatures that were brought to New Zealand were destructive. The sheep and the cow have become the pivot of the country's economic prosperity, and some forms of deer and wild pig roam the high country and provide sportsmen with game for their rifles at weekends. There are even some American elk, which fortunately seem not to have acquired the formidable reputation for causing road accidents that their less responsible Scandinavian cousins have in Sweden, where road signs warning of elks crossing are as common as the wreckage of cars whose drivers found such a hazard difficult to credit.

Wherever you look in the splendidly varied and colourful countryside of this staggeringly beautiful country in the closing years of the twentieth century, it is regrettably but almost certainly true that you see virtually none of New Zealand's native creatures easily. Instead you will see the dominant species of the world outside – the rabbit, the grey squirrel, even the sparrow. But if you have the time, and the patience, and are prepared to take a little advice on where to look, it pays to persevere and seek out some of the most delightfully unusual animals and birds the world has to offer. Finding the

country's native flora is much easier. In recent years, encouraged by the National Parks programme, the New Zealand native trees have made something of a come-back, and one can, particularly in the Fiordland area of the South Island, discover something of the lush, jungle-like forests that used once to cover most of these islands.

The Lakes and Rivers

Nowhere are the contrasts of nature in New Zealand seen more clearly than in the waters of its many lakes and rivers. For the lakes are deep, often tranquil, stretching many miles into the mountainous distance; whereas the rivers tumble and roar as they drain the steep slopes of the peaks of both North and South Islands. Some say that the spirit of New Zealand is to be found where the river meets the lake, for New Zealanders are drawn to water as surely as bears to a bees, nest. Maori and Pakeha alike seek out the great stretches of peaceful lakeland water and the rushing streams and rivers of the mountains; fishing, canoeing, diving, swimming, water-skiing and, in the aerodynamically inclined eighties, wind-surfing.

Appropriately, the country's largest lake is drained by its longest river – the 270-mile long Waikato which brings water from Lake Taupo in the centre of North Island to the Tasman Sea, twenty miles South of the entrance to Manukau Harbour. En route, the Waikato supplies power to the turbines of a number of the hydro-electric power stations that provide New Zealand with its abundant supply of electricity, and supplies water to rich dairy farming areas and several towns. Yet even the Waikato is not New Zealand's largest river in terms of flow and the volume of water that it transports to the ocean. That distinction is claimed by the River Clutha, far to the South in the South Island. The Clutha, which is 210 miles long, drains the dissected Otago plateau, flowing from Lake Wanaka and Lake Hawea, bringing water from the Eastern slopes of the Southern Alps to the Pacific near Kaitangata, some fifty miles South of Dunedin. Like the Waikato in the North, it drives several hydro-electric power stations, and also provides water for the fruit orchards of Otago.

High among the rugged bush-clad hills of the North

Island's Kaimanawa Range, the Rangitikei, over 130 miles long, rises and begins its long descent to the verdant pastures of the lowlands South of Wanganui, a town whose name is shared by another of the North Island's rivers, which also has its source high on the volcanic slopes. Other more slowly flowing, leisurely rivers are to be found on the coastal plains of the Northland peninsula, above Auckland, where the island points to the tropical paradise of the Solomons and another greater island, the second largest in the world – New Guinea. The typical river of the North Island has been, perhaps unfairly, described as "brown-running, stoney and swift... swelling dangerously with Spring anger", but in fact there is a great and exciting variety of colour and texture waiting to be discovered among the rivers of the North.

The South Island has, as well as the Clutha, a number of beautiful and scenically exotic rivers, for the Southern Alps drain both to East and to West, providing long, large and majestic rivers flowing East across the Canterbury Plains and through the hills of Otago, and shorter more tempestuous waterways which flow from the mountains into the Tasman Sea. Particularly worth a visit are the Dart and Rees rivers, which provide water to Lake Wakatipu from the Humboldt, Harris and Richardson ranges of mountains. Here the visual comparison with Norway is at its most striking, for the deep, strong-running rivers swirl powerfully through ancient glacial valleys with steep forbidding sides. On the West coast, the fast-flowing torrents speeding through the gorges of the Buller and Otira provide the recklessly dashing water of the splendid waterfalls of the Fiordland sounds, one of the greatest sights of New Zealand. Yet not all the spectacular waterfalls are in the South Island. For sheer power and spirit, the Aratiatia Rapids and the Huka Falls on the upper reaches of the Waikato, near Lake Taupo, are hard to better.

Yet there is more power, more seemingly controlled muscularity in the mighty, turbulent, eddying rivers of the Canterbury Plains after the Spring thaw than in all the great falls. The seething mass of water that races to the Pacific Ocean through these courses leaves in its wake gold-bearing alluvial deposits which became in the nineteenth century the focus of a gold rush to rival the scramble in the Yukon. The gold found in the 1860s in Otago, around Nelson and along the West Coast was an important factor in the rapid economic growth of New Zealand at the end of the nineteenth century, and in the still young country's financial ability to become the world's pioneer in the concept of the welfare state. Even now, there is still the occasional prospector seeking his fortune with his pan in the water. For New Zealand is an egalitarian society, independent yet caring; capitalist and entre-preneurial without being class-conscious and divisive. No brief discussion of this delightful country could be complete without some consideration of one of its greatest assets – the unique character of the Kiwis themselves. So let us move on to look at the society that has created its past and its future in little more than a hundred years.

The People

A prevalent view of the New Zealand people is summed up by the story of an Australian editor who, with more than the usual measure of brash arrogance so often characteristic of his nation, suggested that a suitable sentence for Australian criminals might be for them to be sent for an extended term in New Zealand without the option of a fine. To those accustomed to societies which encourage and foster wide extremes of viewpoint, and which harbour strong divisions of class or status, New Zealand seems unnaturally uniform, even mediocre. For the people of New Zealand are almost universally middle-class, if it is possible to be middle-class when there is no upper and no lower class between which to fall. They are also more closely attached to the British way of life than the people of any other Commonwealth country. Until quite recently, New Zealanders were almost universally Christian and, to a large extent, active members of a church. New Zealand seems to many outsiders to be a country of limited ambition; of universally small-town aspirations; devoted to the pursuit of comfortable routine, weekend recreation, and the least possible bother. In support of this contention, they point to the lack of cultural activity, the near-absence of commercial theatre, the primness and closeness of provincial life.

Yet, although there are undoubtedly germs of truth in all these stereotypes, there is a much greater truth in the view that the greatest single characteristic of the New Zealander is undemonstrative independence; a lack of the compelling urge felt by the people of so many other nations to show themselves to be fashionable, avant garde, the leaders of opinion. Like the Victorian middle-class in Britain which it has so often been depicted as resembling, New Zealand society has for decades been sure of itself, unquestioningly accepting concepts of right and wrong, propriety, the moral value of hard work and the requirement to help one's neighbour. Yet, unlike the worthies of Victorian England, New Zealand seemed on the surface to maintain those values without losing the ability to have fun. The result was a country which on the one hand led the world in the introduction of universal welfare for the sick, the unemployed and the elderly, and on the other became one of the world's greatest exponents of the outdoor life. It also became a country in which gambling, beer consumption and births out of wedlock all hit extremely high figures per thousand population, and in which the consumption of sleeping pills to cope with stress was way above the average. In short, like Victorian England, this was a society of paradoxes; of high moral values and low resistance to the temptations that threatened them.

Since the mid-seventies, there has been a noticeable shift in thinking and lifestyle among New Zealanders, a greater polarisation of political and social thought and a significant increase in Americanised attitudes and behaviour, presumably created by the all-pervasive influence of US television and media coverage of world events. New Zealanders are becoming more like the rest of us, which may or may not be a good thing, according to your viewpoint. The country's foreign policy now makes the headlines because, almost for the first time, its government holds policies that are no longer middle-of-the-road. The Maori population in Auckland is openly resenting, almost for the first time since the mid-nineteenth century, what its leaders see as its second-rate citizenship, and New Zealand is beginning on a small scale to experience some of the problems of racial friction, heightened by the influx of Polynesian workers from the South Pacific islands where the inhabitants have New Zealand citizenship – the Cook Islands, the Tokelau Islands and Niue. All around the country, the old balance which created one of the world's only truly egalitarian conservative societies is beginning to go awry, and, in the process, the society is becoming more open, in some ways more honest, and in others less attractive.

The welfare state is all-embracing. As well as retirement pensions, introduced as early as 1898, family benefits, first made available in 1926, invalid benefits, introduced in 1936 and the first Social Security Act of 1938 which brought in universal superannuation and a comprehensive state medical system, there is universal public education, a cheap government loan scheme for house purchase, and extensive legislation aimed at the maintenance of a high rate of employment coupled with a good minimum wage. Treatment at all public hospitals is free of charge, as are medicines dispensed against doctors' prescriptions, and the state also pays a significant proportion of the cost of general practitioner care. As in most other countries which have created such total state welfare protection, notably Sweden and the United Kingdom, the economy is beginning to show the strain, and it remains to be seen how well the New Zealand government will do with its difficult task of sustaining the welfare state without drastic increases in public borrowing and inflation.

How the Country is Run

The Head of State in New Zealand is the Queen, known since 1974 by the title Queen of New Zealand. She is represented by a Governor-General who wields no executive power, since this is in the hands of the Executive Council, consisting of the Cabinet, usually made up of about twenty members, advising the Governor-General. The Cabinet is answerable to the House of Representatives, which has only one chamber of eighty-seven members, one per constituency, elected by universal adult suffrage. Any one Member of Parliament in the ruling party therefore has about a forty per cent chance of a Cabinet post, compared with a seven per cent chance in the British House of Commons, and, once in the Cabinet, can expect to be obliged to juggle several portfolios at once. Four of the eighty-seven seats in the House of Representatives are held by Maoris on behalf of the Maori population, one of the last provisions of the original 1852 constitution to remain intact and unaltered.

Elections must be held at least once every three years, and for this reason virtually every Parliament runs its full term. All New Zealand adults over 18 years old must register to vote, and people who are of more than 50% Maori origin must register on the rolls for the Maori seats. Voting itself is not compulsory, and is carried out by crossing out the names of the candidates the voter does not support, rather than the more usual means of placing an X beside the name of the favoured candidate. There are two major political parties, the National Party and the Labour Party, the former the party of free enterprise and the latter the political wing of the Trade Union movement, although the distinction between them is not nearly as sharply defined as that between the Conservative and Labour Parties in Britain. The difference is more one of approach than policy, and is akin to the less than obvious distinctions between the Democratic and Republican Parties in the United States. The former Social Credit Party changed its name during the mid-eighties to the New Zealand Democratic Party, and holds at the time of writing (1985) two seats in the House.

Local government is organised around a two-tier structure, counties and municipalities, most of the municipalities being boroughs. Unlike its equivalents in Britain or the United States, New Zealand local government has few executive and relatively few spending functions, the major county and municipal responsibilities being the provision of the basic utilities, such as electricity, water, and the disposal of sewage and rubbish, with public transport sometimes locally administered and, conversely, the utilities in some areas controlled by autonomous boards. Education is entirely administered and financed by central government. The local authorities, like the House of Representatives, are elected every three years, but largely apolitically, since party politics intrude upon the local government structure only in the cities.

The legal system is based upon British Common Law and, in the absence of a New Zealand law or precedent, British precedents prevail. There are three courts, the lowest level being a stipendiary magistrates' court, the next being the Supreme Court, and the highest the Court of Appeal, although New Zealand citizens do have the right of appeal to the Privy Council in certain cases. Like Britain, New Zealand has an unarmed police force, but, less like Britain, an apparently almost totally law-abiding female population, for there are fewer than 200 places for women in the country's prisons.

Undoubtedly, there are some signs of weakening of New Zealand's moralistic and law-abiding outlook, which may in the end be to the country's benefit. One senses that New Zealanders take all such changes and problems in their stride, continuing to enjoy their beautiful country energetically and with an individualistic flair for the outdoor life. Many young New Zealanders who find the country too restrictive and lacking in opportunity leave their native country for Europe or America each year, and the late seventies and early eighties saw a mass migration of New Zealand youth which reduced the country's population by hundreds of thousands. However, this drift away has been stabilised, and departures are now more or less balanced by the influx of immigrants wanting to capture the unique quality of life that New Zealand can offer. For, as it is to be hoped this book will in a small way have shown, this is a country with so many advantages, so much scenic beauty, so many physical challenges to offer, that it will always remain an ideal environment for those who enjoy pitting themselves against something more than the perils of city life.

Previous page: the dense undergrowth of the Waipoua Kauri Forest, one of the few extensive stands of mature kauri left. The park contains 2,500 hectares of these giant trees, which may stand 50 metres tall and be nearly 2,000 years old. Facing page: (top) Ninety Mile Beach, north of Kaitaia, and (bottom) dusk at Paihia, once home to the missionary Williams brothers, one of whom compiled a Maori dictionary and translated the New Testament into the native tongue. Top: two views of Mangonui, on Doubtless Bay, which began life as a port exporting kauri. Above: farmland near Pakiri. Left: the beautiful land around Matauri Bay. Overleaf: the orchards around Kerikeri, which date back to an intensive development scheme of the 1920s.

Right: a shop at Paihia. Above right: pleasure boats moored in Whangaroa Harbour. In 1809 the harbour witnessed an attack by Maoris on the ship *Boyd*, which they burnt to the waterline, and the death of all but four of the crew. Above: the Stone Store at Kerikeri, which was built in the 1830s, the extravagance of whose construction caused much controversy at the time. Top: yachts anchored at Kerikeri. The rich orchards of Kerikeri (facing page, bottom) thrive in a climate ideal for citrus and kiwi fruits, but need regular spraying by helicopter (facing page, top). Overleaf: the rocky headland of Day Point and Kerikeri Inlet.

Facing page, top: cockle collectors search in the Waitangi River at sunset. Facing page, bottom: a marlin boat docking at Paihia after a day's fishing. Top left: the Shipwreck Museum at Waitangi. Top right: cruise boats moored to the pier at Paihia. Above: dusk settles over the pier of the Bay of Islands Yacht Club, silhouetting the masts of the moored yachts. Left: the Treaty House, kauri flagstaff and Treaty Grounds at Waitangi, all part of the Waitangi National Reserve. On this site was signed the famous treaty of February 6, 1840, in which many Maori chiefs signed sovereignty of the North Island over to Queen Victoria. Overleaf: a view of Russell from Flagstaff Hill.

Russell (these pages) is one of the largest and most picturesque towns on the Bay of Islands. Right: the craft-studded waters of Kororareka Bay. Below: a cruise boat moors at the Wharf. Bottom: Pompallier House, one of Russell's foremost attractions. Though never home to Bishop Pompallier, the house has had a long and chequered career since its construction in 1841. It originally served as a printing shop, survived the sacking of the town by Maoris in 1845 to become a tannery, and is now a museum. Facing page: (top) the Strand and (bottom) a view of the town from Flagstaff Hill.

Below and facing page, top: Urupukapuka Island, where the American author Zane Grey camped in the 1920s, is close to excellent deep-sea fishing and is the site of the exclusive hotel (facing page, bottom) on Otehei Bay. Left: Captain Cook's anchorage off Motuarohia Island. Overleaf: a broad bay on Moturua Island. In 1772 Marion du Fresne established a shore base on the island and buried a bottle decorated with the arms of France which contains a document claiming the land for the French crown.

Facing page, top: the muddy
waters of the boat harbour in
Whangarei, the only city in
Northland. Opua (remaining
pictures) is a small town on
Veronica Channel, part of the
Bay of Islands, which is
linked to Russell by ferry.
Left and facing page, bottom:
the wharf at Waimangaroa
Point. Above: the store and
(top and above left) the
harbour. Overleaf: scenes from
the Round the Bays race, part
of the Fiesta, a fun run of
ten and a half kilometres
around Auckland.

Auckland is the largest city in the nation: (previous pages) Auckland's wharves along Quay Street; (top left) yachts in Okahu Boat Harbour; (top right) Jellicoe Wharf and the Auckland Railway Station; (above) Auckland Harbour Bridge, completed in 1959 after thirty years of discussion and argument. Within ten years of completion traffic had trebled and work had to be undertaken to increase the capacity of the bridge. Right: the greenery of Auckland Domain, with the prominent white walls of the War Memorial Museum; (facing page, top) Waitemata Harbour; (facing page, bottom) One Tree Hill in Cornwall Park, one of the most impressive *pa* to survive to the present day and (overleaf) the serried ranks of yachts in Westhaven Marina and Boat Harbour.

Auckland: (top left) an evening view of the buildings on Quay Street from Ferry Berth; (above) a spectacular fireworks display over Mission Bay; (top right) lights flicker among the moored yachts of Westhaven Marina at dusk; (above right) lights illuminate the front of Auckland Railway Station and the cranes of Freyberg Wharf beyond; (right) the rays of the setting sun silhouette the dockyard cranes and the high-rise buildings of Auckland City, and (bottom right) a Russian cruise ship berthed at Princess Wharf emphasises the international flavour of Auckland.

Auckland: (top left) a distant view of the city from Kohimarama to the east; (top right) north of One Tree Hill lies Alexandra Park with its Trotting Course and A and P Showgrounds; one of the longest and safest beaches on Waitemata Harbour is Kohimarama Beach (above), backed along its entire length by Tamaki Drive; elsewhere, Tamaki Drive skirts Mission Bay (right), where a museum is devoted to Melanesian artefacts; (facing page, top) St Heliers Bay, which boasts a fine beach and a memorial to *HMS Achilles*, a New Zealand warship which helped defeat the German battleship *Graf Spee* in 1939; (facing page, bottom) the War Memorial Museum, which contains many exhibits other than its war relics and (overleaf) the stumpy Ferry Berth in front of the Air New Zealand Building.

Auckland: (top) a banner strung across Queen Street and bright lights proclaim the Civic Theatre; (above) the modern architecture and design of the Downtown Shopping Centre off Albert Street; (above right and right) participants in the 'Ironman' Triathlon, a competition of running, swimming and cycling held in Auckland; (facing page, bottom) fishermen on Orakei Wharf and (overleaf) Okahu Boat Harbour, with the curving causeway of Tamaki Drive and the straight causeway of the North Island Main Trunk Railway cutting Hobson Bay off from the ocean. Facing page, top: the mighty Lion Rock at Piha, on the coast west of Auckland.

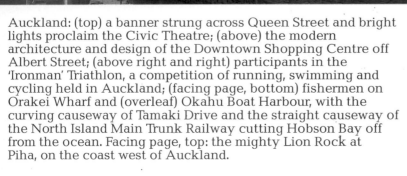

The Coromandel Peninsula (these pages) contains some of the loveliest scenery in the North Island: (facing page, top) Otama Beach, near the old gold-town of Kuaotunu; (facing page, bottom) Whiritoa Beach, ideal for surf-casting; (top) Kuaotunu Beach; (above) sunset over the Coromandel Range; (above left) the Black Jack Scenic Reserve and (left) palm trees that line Buffalo Beach at Whitianga. Further south lie the mist-shrouded rocks (overleaf) near Tauranga.

The small town of Coromandel, (left) the fishing wharf, took its name from the first ship to visit the harbour. Three kilometres south stands the All Saints Church (top). Thames, which found its early prosperity in gold mining, can boast both St James' Church (above left) and the Church of St George the Martyr (above). Facing page, bottom: children fishing near Tauranga. Facing page, top: sheep grazing near Manaia, on the Coromandel Peninsula. Overleaf: Tudor Towers at Rotorua.

Facing page, top: Tudor Towers was built in 1907 bringing elegance to the thermal spa town of Rotorua, an elegance further enhanced by the bowling club on Hinemaru Street (centre left and centre right). Facing page, bottom: the shops along Victoria Street in Hamilton, a town named after Captain Hamilton, who died fighting the Maoris in 1864. Above: the Court House in Hamilton. Top: the broad Victoria Street in Cambridge, a town which boasts a green where cricket is often played and the graceful St Andrew's church (left).

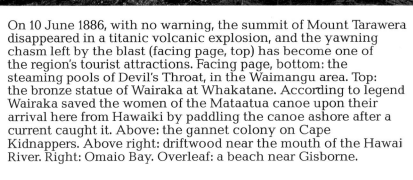

On 10 June 1886, with no warning, the summit of Mount Tarawera disappeared in a titanic volcanic explosion, and the yawning chasm left by the blast (facing page, top) has become one of the region's tourist attractions. Facing page, bottom: the steaming pools of Devil's Throat, in the Waimangu area. Top: the bronze statue of Wairaka at Whakatane. According to legend Wairaka saved the women of the Mataatua canoe upon their arrival here from Hawaiki by paddling the canoe ashore after a current caught it. Above: the gannet colony on Cape Kidnappers. Above right: driftwood near the mouth of the Hawai River. Right: Omaio Bay. Overleaf: a beach near Gisborne.

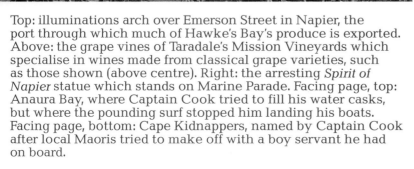

Top: illuminations arch over Emerson Street in Napier, the
port through which much of Hawke's Bay's produce is exported.
Above: the grape vines of Taradale's Mission Vineyards which
specialise in wines made from classical grape varieties, such
as those shown (above centre). Right: the arresting *Spirit of
Napier* statue which stands on Marine Parade. Facing page, top:
Anaura Bay, where Captain Cook tried to fill his water casks,
but where the pounding surf stopped him landing his boats.
Facing page, bottom: Cape Kidnappers, named by Captain Cook
after local Maoris tried to make off with a boy servant he had
on board.

When part of the Orakei Korako thermal area was flooded behind a dam it was thought that some of the beauty may disappear, but the activity was, if anything, increased: (top and facing page, bottom) the Rainbow Terrace. Waiotapu thermal area lies south of Rotorua and can boast: the Bridal Veil Falls (above left); Champagne Pool (left); Devil's Home (facing page, top) and the famous Lady Knox Geyser (above). This peculiar geyser was not discovered until the turn of the century when prisoners found that soap triggered its spoutings.

Right: the calm waters of Lake Whakamaru, created in the 1950s behind a huge earth and concrete dam. Below and facing page, top: Lake Taupo, a 620-square-kilometre lake which is not only ideal for sailing, but also a superb fishing ground, where three-kilogram trout are a common catch. Bottom right: the lakeside motels of Taupo. Bottom left: the steaming Craters of the Moon near Taupo. Facing page, bottom: part of the Wairakei Geothermal Power Project which brings steam and hot water up from the depths to power turbines which have a total generating capacity of 192,600 kilowatts.

Left and below: the steaming crater lake atop Mount Ruapehu, which was not seen until the peak was scaled by George Beetham in 1879. Right: Ruapehu with Mount Egmont visible as a tiny peak on the far horizon. According to legend Mount Egmont had to flee westwards after fighting with his rival in love, Tongariro, seen in the foreground (bottom left) together with the symmetrical Ngauruhoe and towering Ruapehu. Bottom right: the holiday town of Acacia Bay on Lake Taupo.

The towering bulk of Mount Egmont (top, above right, right and facing page, bottom) dominates the entire region about its foot. Though it has not erupted since white settlement began, it is thought to have erupted in about 1630, and many think it may do so again. Above: newly-shorn sheep near Uruti, northeast of Mount Egmont. Above right: a locomotive in Inglewood, a town of some 2,500 inhabitants which services the surrounding farmland. Facing page, top: the brightly coloured cliffs of the Onaero Scenic Reserve on the North Taranaki Bight.

This page: (right) the view along the Rimutka Pass. When, in 1878, it was proposed to push a railway inland from Wellington, it was the severity of this incline which forced the engineers to employ the Fell engine, a specialist locomotive developed by John Fell, which continued in use for eighty years. Below right: the Good Shepherd Anglican church at Tinui. It was at Tinui that the first Anzac Day ceremony was held in 1916. The steaming cliffs of Waimangu (bottom right) testify to the instability of the Rotorua area, which has been wracked by volcanic eruptions many times. The waters of the area are too hot for fish, but ideal for the growth of algae (below).

Facing page, top: New Plymouth, where the first few European settlers became entangled in a local Maori war and had to hold out against an army from Waikato. Today, the city has developed a variety of industries and is one of the world's major exporters of cheese. It is perhaps best known for the oil and gas found in the vicinity, which provides an important source of fuel for the nation. Facing page, bottom: the city of Wanganui, one of the oldest in New Zealand. In the course of Maori inter-tribal wars of the last century, some 1,500 warriors came down the river and slaughtered the Wanganui Maoris, indulging in a huge cannibal feast to celebrate their victory.

Above: surfers wade out to sea at Paraparaumu, a commuter settlement some 50 miles north of Wellington. Top left: Kaoroi Rock Lighthouse and (right) nearby coastline. Top right: a surfer dashes to shore past the dramatic rock formations of Castlepoint. Above right: the Castlepoint Lighthouse, which was erected in 1913 and stands some 170 feet above the waves, a drop which killed one of the keepers in 1922. Far right: the looming presence of Castle Rock broods over a broad beach popular with surfers, bathers and family groups alike. Overleaf: yachts moored in Oriental Bay, Wellington.

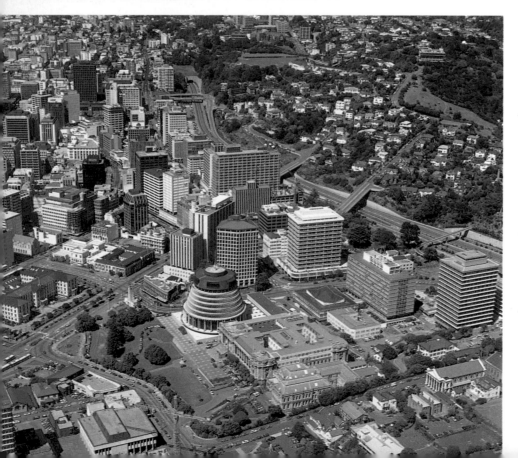

Previous pages: Wellington, with the Railway Station, Parliament Buildings and high-rise buildings of the central region. Top left: crowds gather to watch the Nissan Sport, a 500-kilometre motor race through the streets of Wellington. Centre left: a night-time view across Lambton Harbour towards Oriental Parade. Bottom left: the distinctive, conical Beehive, which houses executive offices, stands beside the columned Parliament Buildings of 1922, the General Assembly Library of 1897 and the red-roofed Government Buildings. The latter is generally acknowledged to be the second largest wooden building in the world, and if its kauri cladding is shaped to resemble stone, this does not detract from the beauty of the structure. Above: the container ships *Union Auckland* and *Union Sydney* dock before the black tower of the Bank of New Zealand Building, the tallest structure in the city. Right: Point Dorset Beach. Overleaf: Oriental Parade runs beside the waters of Lambton Harbour, past the breakwaters of Freyberg Pool and into the city.

With over three thousand inhabitants, Picton (these pages) is a thriving town on Queen Charlotte Sound. Top left: Oxley's Hotel, on the corner of London Quay and Wellington Street. Top right: High Street. Centre: the Yacht Harbour. Above: palm trees along the waterfront. Right: London Quay. Facing page: two early-morning views of the Yacht Harbour.

Right, below, below right and facing page, bottom: the beautiful, pure sands of Kaiteriteri, a tiny settlement on the western shores of Tasman Bay, long famous for its beach, which is often packed with holidaymakers. Bottom left: the tranquil waters of Sandy Bay, whence the marble was shipped to Wellington for the construction of the Parliament Buildings. Bottom right: a car from another era trundles along Nelson's Trafalgar Street, named after the greatest victory of the city's namesake. The city makes its living from the resources of the surrounding area, exporting the fruit and forestry products of the countryside together with fish from the ocean. Facing page, top: the dark mass of Fifeshire Rock, in Tasman Bay.

Facing page, top: a stranded wreck slowly disintegrates in the waters off Motueka. Facing page, bottom: the Kaikoura Peninsula where, according to legend, Maui braced himself when he hauled the North Island up from the depths. Left: spume retreats across the dark sands of Conway Flat Beach. Below: a distant view of the Bryant Range and Tasman Bay from the slopes of Takaka Hill. Bottom left: an evening scene near Motueka. Bottom right: the Waiau River, with the Kaikoura Mountains beyond. Overleaf: Christchurch.

Christchurch (these pages and overleaf) had its origins in a Church of England settlement whose members were required to produce a letter from their vicar testifying to their good character, and is now a city of 300,000 people and many denominations. Top and right: the tree-lined Avon River winds through the city. Above: the bandstand on the banks of the Avon, next to Manchester Street Bridge. Above right: the modern City Mall off Colombo Street. Far right: the Bridge of Remembrance, opened on 11 November 1924 by the Governor General, Lord Jellicoe, to replace that over which so many men marched to join in the First World War. Facing page: Cathedral Square and Christchurch Cathedral, which was begun in 1864 but not completed until 40 years later, is one of the city's major focal points.

Above: Charteris Bay Golf Course, backed by the bulk of Mount Herbert. Above right: a wooden ramp leads down into the waters of Cass Bay, west of Lyttelton. Right: rowing boats on a pier at Purau Bay, best known for its sheltered beaches. Below and facing page, bottom: fishing boats moored in Lyttelton Harbour, a long arm of the sea which cuts deep into the neck of Banks Peninsula. Bottom right: a beautiful sunset over Port Lyttelton, as seen from Summit Road. Facing page, top: a view across Lyttelton towards the docks. The town lies in a vast volcanic crater which ceased to erupt many ages ago. When the sea broke in it created a marvellous natural harbour, which remains the best sea-route into Canterbury and one of the busiest ports in the nation.

Top left and facing page, top: the grasslands of the South Canterbury Plains. Top right: sheep descend to drink from a small stream near Pigeon Bay, one of the long inlets which reach into Banks Peninsula. Above: sheep graze on the rich land beneath the Mount Hutt Range, southwest of Christchurch. The road between Teddington and Motukarara climbs over Geddies Pass (right) and effectively cuts across the neck of Banks Peninsula. As well as Lyttelton, Banks Peninsula contains the flooded volcano known as Akaroa Bay, of which Duvauchelle Bay (facing page, bottom) is a part. Overleaf: the downs around Fairlie.

The first viable route to the west coast north of the Southern Alps is that which passes over Arthur's Pass and descends by way of the scenic Otira Gorge (previous pages). Facing page: Point Elizabeth, north of Greymouth. Top left: driftwood and a stranded fishing boat at Hokitika. Top right: cricket on the Town Green of Greymouth, which now thrives on the timber trade. Left: Greymouth's Mackay Street, named after the man who negotiated the purchase of much of Westland from the Maori. Above: the Pancake Rocks at Punakaiki. Overleaf: rocks near Greymouth.

The mountains of the South
Island (previous and these
pages and overleaf) are
amongst the most spectacular
in the Pacific. Previous
pages: a meltwater stream
tumbles from the foot of the
Franz Josef Glacier. Right:
Mount Cook rising above the
clouds. Below: the Southern
Alps. Below right: the Tasman
Glacier. Bottom: Lake
Matheson. Facing page, top:
the mighty, 13-kilometre-long
Fox Glacier. Both the Fox and
the Franz Josef lie in
Westland National Park and are
amongst the chief attractions
of the region. However,
following a trend visible in
glaciers throughout the world,
the two are slowly retreating
as climatic conditions change.
Facing page, bottom: the
towering, 3,764-metre-tall
bulk of Mount Cook, reflected
in the waters of Lake Pukaki.
Overleaf: hikers crossing the
Fletcher Bridge.

Facing page: the Fox Glacier, named after Sir William Fox who visited the area as Premier, with the great icefields and the 3,066-metre peak of Mount Tasman beyond. Top: the meltwaters of the Franz Josef Glacier run down to meet the Waiho River, their milkiness the result of the vast amount of rock dust ground by the glacier. Above: the seemingly fragile Douglas Bridge crosses the meltwater of the Franz Josef Glacier west of Franz Josef town. Right: the deep U-shaped valley left by the retreating Franz Josef, so typical of previously glaciated landscapes. Overleaf: a mountaineer's hut on a crag beneath Mount Tasman.

The massive Southern Alps (these pages) form an almost impenetrable barrier to communication between the west coast and the rest of South Island. From Lake Wakatipu 320 kilometres north to Arthur's Pass, only the route over the Gates of Haast provides access. Left: a boulder-strewn river-bed beneath Mount Cook. Bottom left: the Hooker Valley. Bottom right: the milky waters of Lake Tekapo provides superb trout fishing. Below: the high peaks around Mount Cook.

Top left: the rocky summits of the Southern Alps south of Mount Cook, whose snow-capped peak is shown (top right). Above: the smooth surface of the high snowfields above the Franz Josef Glacier. It is here that the snow collects and is compacted into ice before becoming a part of the glacier. Right and facing page, top: the rugged scenery around Mount Tasman. Facing page, bottom: the jagged surface of the upper portion of the Fox Glacier and Mount Tasman. Overleaf, left: Bruce Bay, once the centre of a violent riot when 3,000 miners were tricked by Albert Hunt, the famous prospector. Overleaf, top right: Knights Point, north of Haast. Overleaf, bottom right: Lake Hawea which, according to legend, has a magical floating island.

Top left: Main Street in Arrowtown, once a gold-rush town and now the centre of a small farming region. To the west, just north of Queenstown, is the Golden Terrace Mining Village (top right), a recreation of the gold-rush days of a century ago. Above: Queenstown, a town with a population of over 3,000, has become one of the nation's most popular resorts. It nestles in a beautiful setting between Lake Wakatipu and the mountains and was named, the story goes, after miners pronounced it fit for any queen. Right: small sailing craft by Lake Wakatipu. Facing page: Queenstown Harbour. Overleaf: nearby scenery.

These pages: the colourful costumes and floats of the Dunedin Carnival procession as it makes its way along Princes and George Streets. Overleaf: an aerial view of Dunedin's Octagon, with the Gothic St Paul's Cathedral.

Top left: Dunedin's Carisbrook Cricket Ground, a venue for Test and other matches. Top right: the Dunedin Botanical Gardens, an island of tranquillity amid the city bustle, off Opoho Road. Above: some of the fine docking facilities and the railway yards which have made the city an important industrial port. Right: the farmland around Mosgiel which, like the townsite itself, was recovered from extensive swamps. Facing page, top: Dunedin's magnificent beach at St Kilda. Facing page, bottom: Forbury Park racecourse, in Dunedin's southern suburbs.

Dunedin: (top) a golden sunset over St Clair Beach, on the city's southern shore; (above) St Paul's Anglican Cathedral, completed in 1915 after years of disagreement and discussion; (right) the statue of Donald MacNaughton Stuart, Minister of Knox Chruch from 1860 to 1894, in Queen's Gardens. Above right: Knot Garden, (facing page, top) the Glasshouse and (facing page, bottom) the Duck Pond, all in the city's colourful Botanical Gardens.

The Otago Peninsula (these pages) juts eastwards into the Pacific Ocean from Dunedin and contains some of the most romantic scenery in the area: (facing page, top) the sweeping curve of Victory Beach and the tidal entrance to Papanui Inlet as seen from the headland of Titi Koraki; (facing page, bottom and below left) Sandfly Bay, on the peninsula's southern shore, where Lion Rock lies just offshore together with the nearby Gull Rocks; (left) the waters of Otago Harbour, looking towards Port Chalmers, the peninsula's deep water port, from above Raynbirds Bay; (bottom left) the crooked finger of Yellow Head, with the sweep of Broad Bay beyond, and (bottom right) the sheer cliffs of Maori Head, with Bird Island and the sands of Smails Beach beyond.

Top: the setting sun casts long shadows over the hills near Cromwell. Above: the Clutha River tumbles through a gorge on the first stage of its long journey to reach the Pacific near Kaitangata. Above right: the Kakanui Mountains which close the southern edge of the Waitaki River valley. Right: Glendhu Bay, one of the most tranquil spots on Lake Wanaka. Nestled between the Knobby and Old Man ranges, and stretching along the Clutha River, is one of the most important orchard areas in the country, and all around Roxburgh vast orchards (facing page) fill the landscape.

Facing page: Lake Wakatipu, (top) at Queenstown and (bottom) from the Remarkables, is the site of a strange phenomenon. On occasion, the level of water in the lake rhythmically rises and falls. Maoris ascribed this to the beating of a giant's heart deep in the lake, but scientists term it a seiche, attributable to wind or atmospheric pressure. Top left and above: the Remarkables, a sharp ridge which lies south of Queenstown. Left and top right: the now-quiet Shotover River which runs from Lochnagar to Lake Wakatipu. In November 1862 two sheep-shearers struck gold in the Shotover and started a gold rush. Overleaf: Milford Sound is both one of the most dramatic and one of the most visited of the fiords on the southwest coast of South Island.

Previous pages: the South Fiord of Lake Te Anau, with Lake Hilda beyond its end. Top, right and facing page: the majestic beauties of Milford Sound, to which the Maoris came in search of the much-prized 'tear-drop' greenstone, but which is now visited simply for its grandeur. Above: Mirror Lakes, near Lake Te Anau. Above right: the distant Middle Fiord of Lake Te Anau from the southwest. Overleaf: lush pasture near Lake Hauroko.

Top: Lake Te Anau, the largest lake on the South Island.
Above: petrified tree-stumps amid the seaweed at Curio Bay.
Above right: Bluff, a port on the Southland coast. Right: a
floatplane taxis on the lake at the town of Te Anau. Facing
page, top: the town of Te Anau from above the lake. Facing
page, bottom: the River Waiau, which flows from Lake Te
Anau to Lake Manapouri and thence to the sea at Te Waewae
Bay. Overleaf: Lake Hankinson, with Lake Te Anau beyond.